THE
TOTALLY
APPLES
COOKBOOK

THE
TOTALLY
APPLES
COOKBOOK

By Helene Siegel & Karen Gillingham

Illustrated by Carolyn Vibbert

CELESTIAL ARTS
BERKELEY, CALIFORNIA

The Totally Apples Cookbook is produced by becker&mayer!, Ltd.

Printed in Singapore.

Cover design and illustration: Bob Greisen
Interior design and typesetting: Susan Hernday
Interior illustrations: Carolyn Vibbert

Library of Congress Cataloging-in-Publication Data
Siegel, Helene.
    The Totally Apples Cookbook / by Helene Siegel.
        p.   cm.
    ISBN-13: 978-0-89087-883-5
    ISBN-10: 0-89087-883-8
    1. Cookery (Apples)   I. Title.
TX813.A6S54   1998
641.6'411—dc21   98-24749
                        CIP

Celestial Arts Publishing
P.O. Box 7123
Berkeley, CA 94707

Look for all the *Totally* books at your local store!

CONTENTS

INTRODUCTION

This is a happy moment for apples! After a short fling with kiwis and some ardent glances at passion fruit, Americans seem to have come to their senses and returned to the apple—a fruit we can count on.

The American love affair with apples goes back to colonial times, when they grew in such abundance that apple pie was even eaten as a meal. Apples have been bobbed for at Halloween parties, passed under chins at county fairs, given to stern teachers to warm their hearts, and polished by sycophants.

They have been squeezed into cider to make the favorite beverage of colonial times, and sold on street corners to get by during the Great Depression. In short, they have been America's favorite fruit for over two hundred years.

Though apples may have tried our patience in the recent past by being overly red, waxed, uniform, and at times disappointingly mealy, we seem to have turned a corner. Today, a walk down the aisle of a good supermarket's produce section yields a tasty display of tart green Grannies, tender, pale Pink Ladies, yellow and red-striped Galas, fragrant Braeburns, bright red Romes, and enough heart-shaped Red Delicious apples to make your heart stop—or at least make you entertain the possibility of bagging a few and heading home to bake a pie.

And if baking a pie seems too daunting, we have a few other ideas to get those juices flowing: salads and sandwiches that highlight the apple's crispness; baked and roasted dishes that give the apple's sugar a chance to caramelize and mellow; beverages to warm the soul; and plenty of sweet, wholesome desserts. From old-fashioned brown bettys, crisps, and crumbles to new-fangled granitas and crystallized ginger upside-down cakes, the goodness of apples always shines through!

"An apple a day keeps the doctor away."
          —proverb

SEVERAL SALADS
AND
A SOUP

RED APPLE AND WALNUT SALAD

What a great way to perk up winter appetites—a cold, crisp salad with nuts, apples, and creamy buttermilk dressing!

5 heads Belgian endive, thinly sliced crosswise
1 unpeeled Red Delicious apple, cored and cut in matchsticks
$2/3$ cup walnuts, toasted and chopped in chunks
$1/4$ cup crumbled blue cheese
$1/2$ cup low-fat buttermilk
$1/4$ cup red wine vinegar
2 teaspoons honey
salt and freshly ground pepper

In a large bowl, toss together endive, apple, walnuts, and blue cheese.

In a small bowl, whisk together buttermilk, vinegar, honey, salt, and pepper. Pour enough dressing over salad to coat lightly. Mix well and serve.

SERVES 4 TO 6

Apples in Salads and Sandwiches
For adding crackle and snap to sandwiches and salads, we like a firm apple with some personality. Slice thinly, and leave on the skin for added crunch and color. Granny Smith, Red Delicious, Fuji, Gala, and Winesap are all terrific.

CURRIED APPLE BISQUE

Serve this delicate soup in small bowls at the start of an elegant dinner party.

2 tablespoons butter
1 onion, chopped
1 celery stalk, chopped
2 Fuji apples, peeled, cored, and finely
    chopped
2 teaspoons curry powder
1 teaspoon ground coriander
$\frac{1}{2}$ teaspoon sugar
$\frac{1}{4}$ teaspoon turmeric
4 cups chicken stock
$\frac{1}{4}$ cup uncooked white rice
salt and freshly ground pepper
$\frac{1}{2}$ cup half-and-half
fresh cilantro sprigs, for garnish

Melt the butter in a stockpot over medium heat. Add onion and celery and sauté until soft, about 5 minutes. Add apples, curry, coriander, sugar, and turmeric. Turn up heat, stir well, and cook 5 minutes.

Pour in chicken stock and rice. Bring to a boil, then reduce to a simmer. Cover and cook, 15 minutes, until rice is done and apples are tender. Transfer to a blender and purée until smooth. Return to the pot, season to taste, and bring nearly to a boil. Stir in half-and-half, cook briefly to heat through, and serve. Garnish with cilantro sprigs if desired.

SERVES 4 TO 6

CRUNCHY APPLE BACON SALAD

Apples are a good foil for the rich taste of bacon. This salad makes a nice small lunch.

1 medium head romaine lettuce, torn in
  bite-size pieces
1 large Fuji *or* Gala apple, peeled, cored, and
  cut in chunks
4 slices bacon, fried, drained, and crumbled
3/4 cup cheddar cheese cubes
1/4 red onion, thinly sliced
1/4 cup sherry vinegar
1/4 cup vegetable oil
salt and freshly ground pepper

In a large bowl, combine the lettuce, apple, bacon, cheese, and onion. Toss well.

In a small bowl, whisk together vinegar, oil, salt, and pepper. Pour on enough dressing to coat lightly, and toss well. Leftover dressing may be kept in refrigerator.

SERVES 4

CLASSIC CHICKEN SALAD

Chicken-and-apple salad is a sure hit for a ladies' lunch or tea.

2½ pounds boneless chicken breasts
1 celery stalk, diced
2 Granny Smith *or* Fuji apples, peeled, cored, and diced
2 teaspoons capers, drained
¼ cup prepared mayonnaise
1½ tablespoons Dijon mustard
2 tablespoons lemon juice
salt and freshly ground pepper

Poach the chicken breasts for 20 minutes in enough water or stock to cover. Let cool.

Remove skin, and cut chicken into bite-size chunks. Place in mixing bowl. Add celery, apples, capers, mayonnaise, mustard, and lemon juice. Combine well. Season to taste with salt and pepper, and chill.

SERVES 4, OR ENOUGH FOR 3 SANDWICHES

UP-TO-DATE WALDORF

Serve this American classic as a starter at Thanksgiving dinner, or add leftover chopped chicken or turkey for a substantial main-course salad.

1 large unpeeled Golden Delicious apple, cored and roughly chopped
1 (10-ounce) package mixed salad greens
$\frac{1}{2}$ cup thinly sliced celery
$\frac{1}{2}$ cup coarsely chopped walnuts, toasted
$\frac{1}{2}$ cup dried cranberries
$\frac{1}{4}$ cup low-fat sour cream
2 tablespoons honey mustard
2 tablespoons white wine vinegar
$\frac{1}{2}$ teaspoon sugar
salt and freshly ground pepper

In a large bowl, combine apple, salad greens, celery, walnuts, and cranberries. In another bowl, stir together sour cream, mustard, vinegar, and sugar. Season to taste with salt and pepper. Pour over salad, and toss to coat thoroughly. Store in refrigerator.

SERVES 4

The Whole Health Story

The apple's reputation as a health food is well founded. The average apple is 90 percent water, contains 80 calories, and is extremely high in bulk. An apple eaten with the skin on contains more soluble fiber than a bowl of oatmeal. It has no sodium or fat, and plenty of vitamin C in the skin itself. As for the lunchbox set, studies have shown that children who snack on apples have fewer cavities, thanks to the acid in apple pulp.

WINTER FRUIT SALAD

This light, refreshing salad makes an excellent starter or a healthful dessert.

2 Fuji *or* Gala apples, peeled, cored, and
   thinly sliced
1 unpeeled Golden Delicious apple, cored
   and thinly sliced
2 ripe pears, peeled, cored, and thinly sliced
¼ cup sugar
½ cup water
¼ cup Grand Marnier
⅓ cup raisins *or* chopped dried figs
½ cup unsweetened shredded coconut
½ cup toasted almonds, roughly chopped

In a large bowl, combine the apples and pears.

In a small saucepan, combine the sugar and water. Bring to a boil, and simmer until clear. In another small pan, combine Grand Marnier and raisins or figs. Bring to boil, turn off heat, and let steep 5 minutes.

Pour sugar syrup and dried fruit mixture over fruit in bowl. Add coconut and nuts. Toss well, and chill.

SERVES 4

Storing Apples at Home

Apples taste best if stored at room temperature. If you purchase large quantities in plastic bags, store them in a cool part of the house. Remove any spoiled apples, punch some holes in the bag so air can circulate, and eat 'em fast.

APPLE CARROT SALAD

This simple summer salad is best served immediately for maximum crunch and color.

3 large carrots, peeled
2 unpeeled Red Delicious apples
2 tablespoons lemon juice
1 teaspoon honey, or to taste

Grate or shred the carrots and apples—the medium shredding disk on your food processor works fine. Transfer to bowl. Whisk together lemon juice and honey. Pour over salad, and toss well to combine. Serve or chill before serving.

MAKES 1 QUART

"Comfort me with apples; for I am sick of love."
—Bible: *Song of Solomon 2:5*

HONEST-TO-APPLE
ENTRÉES

HONEY-GLAZED PORK LOIN WITH BROWNED APPLES

The time-honored combination of pork and fruit is enhanced with an extra dollop of brown sugar.

MARINADE
1/2 cup orange juice
1/4 cup soy sauce
2 tablespoons vegetable oil
2 garlic cloves, chopped
2 (1/4-inch) slices ginger, chopped
1/2 teaspoon Chinese chile sauce
1 pound pork tenderloin

GLAZE
1/2 cup orange juice
1/2 cup apple cider *or* juice
2 tablespoons soy sauce
3 tablespoons honey

1 tablespoon butter
2 Fuji apples, peeled, cored, and sliced
2 teaspoons brown sugar

Whisk together marinade ingredients.
Place pork in shallow pan or dish, pour on
marinade, and marinate in the refrigerator
4 hours or longer.

In a small saucepan, combine glaze ingredients. Bring to a boil, reduce to a simmer,
and cook 10 minutes.

Preheat oven to 425 degrees F. Transfer
pork to roasting pan, discarding marinade.
Bake for 45 minutes, brushing with glaze
about four times. Cool slightly.

Just before serving, melt butter in a small
skillet over medium-high heat. Sauté apples
with brown sugar until edges are brown, 5 to
10 minutes.

To serve, thinly slice the pork. Arrange on
four serving plates, alongside browned
apples. Top each with a few spoonfuls of
glaze. Serve with remaining glaze in a bowl.

SERVES 4

BRAISED SAUSAGES WITH APPLES

Use savory or spicy, but not sweet, sausages to contrast with the apples in this dish.

2 tablespoons butter
1½ pounds large sausage links
1 onion, thinly sliced
3 Granny Smith apples, peeled, cored, and cut in thick wedges
juice of ½ lemon
2 tablespoons brown sugar
¼ teaspoon cinnamon
dash nutmeg and cloves
salt and freshly ground pepper

Melt butter in a large skillet over medium-high heat. Add sausages and cook, turning frequently, until brown. Remove, and drain on paper towels.

Add onion to pan. Sauté in drippings, stirring frequently, until soft, about 5 minutes.

Add apples and cook about 3 minutes longer, or until apples are tender-crisp and onions golden. Stir in lemon juice, brown sugar, cinnamon, nutmeg, and cloves. Return sausages to skillet, and toss to combine. Cover and cook over low heat 15 to 20 minutes, until sausages are cooked through and apples are soft. Season to taste.

SERVES 4 TO 6

Apple Cooking Tips

- *Three medium apples equals 1 pound.*
- *One pound apples equals 4 cups chopped or diced.*
- *Juice or cider may be used interchangeably in recipes.*
- *Overripe or bruised apples make fine sauce—just cut away the bruised part.*
- *Sprinkle cut apples with lemon juice to slow browning.*

DUCK WITH BRANDIED CHERRIES AND APPLES

Few ingredients spell "special occasion" as well as duck does. Breasts are available at the butcher counter in better supermarkets and in the freezer case at specialty fish-and-poultry stores.

2 tablespoons dried sour cherries
½ cup apple juice
2 tablespoons butter
2 McIntosh *or* Granny Smith apples, peeled, cored, and cut into thick wedges
2 teaspoons sugar
1 tablespoon olive oil
4 boneless duck breast halves
salt and freshly ground pepper
⅓ cup brandy
⅓ cup chicken broth

Soak cherries in apple juice for ½ hour.

In a large skillet, melt the butter over medium heat. Add apples, sprinkle with

sugar, and sauté until golden, about
2 minutes on each side. Remove from pan
and keep warm in oven.

Add oil to pan, and increase heat to medium-high. Season duck breasts all over with
salt and pepper. Add duck breasts, skin-side
down, and sauté until browned, about
5 minutes. Pour off any excess oil. Turn duck
over, and add cherries-and-apple-juice mixture. Stir in brandy and broth. Reduce heat,
cover, and simmer about 10 minutes, or until
duck is done to taste. Remove duck with slotted spoon, and transfer to warm oven.

Increase heat and bring pan juices to boil.
Boil until reduced to ½ cup. Adjust seasonings with salt and pepper. Thinly slice duck
breasts and fan each one on a serving plate.
Arrange apples alongside. Pour hot cherry
sauce over each.

SERVES 4

APPLES
ON
THE SIDE

APPLE RHUBARB SAUCE

If you are tired of that bland sauce sold in the jar, try this chunky, spunky applesauce—guaranteed to brighten whatever is served alongside it.

4 Gala apples, peeled, cored, and cut in chunks
$\frac{1}{2}$ cup frozen rhubarb chunks
$\frac{1}{2}$ cup cold water
$\frac{1}{2}$ cup sugar
3 tablespoons lemon juice
2 cloves

Combine all the ingredients in a heavy saucepan. Bring to a boil, reduce to a simmer, and cook, uncovered, $\frac{1}{2}$ hour, until apples are tender. Remove from heat. Mash with a wooden spoon or fork and remove cloves. Store in the refrigerator for up to two weeks.

MAKES 2 CUPS

GINGER APPLE CHUTNEY

Keep a jar of this sweet and spicy condiment in the refrigerator for jazzing up turkey burgers, roasted duck or chicken, and homemade curries.

2 tablespoons vegetable oil
$\frac{1}{2}$ tablespoon mustard seeds
1 onion, diced
1 red bell pepper, cored, seeded, and diced
1 garlic clove, minced
2 teaspoons minced fresh ginger
4 cloves
1 cinnamon stick, halved
2 dried red chiles, crushed
4 Granny Smith apples, peeled, cored, and chopped
$\frac{1}{4}$ cup raisins
$\frac{1}{2}$ cup brown sugar
$\frac{1}{2}$ cup red wine vinegar
$1\frac{1}{4}$ cups water

In a large, heavy pot, warm the oil over high heat. Add the seeds, cover, and cook until they stop popping. Remove lid and reduce heat to medium-high.

Add the onion and bell pepper, and sauté until soft. Turn up the heat, stir in the garlic and ginger, and cook briefly. Add cloves, cinnamon, and chiles, and cook another minute. Then stir in the apples, raisins, brown sugar, vinegar, and water. (If necessary, add more water to cover.) Simmer, uncovered, until apples are soft but still hold a shape and mixture thickens, 30 to 40 minutes. Remove cinnamon sticks and chill. Store in the refrigerator for up to two weeks.

MAKES 1 QUART

Sauce Apples
Newtown Pippin and Elstar are considered best for making homemade sauce. McIntosh and Granny Smith are two of the authors' personal favorites.

SMASHED APPLES AND CRANBERRIES

Here is a quick and easy side for roasted pork, lamb, or beef.

3 Golden Delicious apples, halved lengthwise and cored
2 cinnamon sticks, broken in thirds
6 cloves
2 tablespoons dried cranberries
$1/4$ cup apple brandy
salt

Preheat oven to 325 degrees F.

Stuff each apple half with a piece of cinnamon and a clove. Place flat-side down in baking pan and bake until soft, 30 to 40 minutes. Cool slightly.

Meanwhile, combine the cranberries and brandy in a small pot. Bring to a boil, remove from heat, and let sit.

Scoop out pulp of cooled apples, and place in a bowl. Discard cinnamon and cloves. Roughly mash with a fork. Add cranberry mixture and a dash of salt, and stir to combine. Serve warm.

SERVES 4

"One bad apple spoils the bunch."
—proverb

ROASTED APPLES AND SWEET POTATOES

A friend's baby-sitter, Marta di Paolo from Colombia, shared this wonderful healthy casserole.

2 large sweet potatoes, halved
2 tablespoons butter
3 Fuji apples, peeled, cored, cut in large
   chunks
1 teaspoon brown sugar
$\frac{1}{2}$ teaspoon salt
$\frac{1}{4}$ teaspoon cinnamon
$\frac{1}{8}$ teaspoon allspice

In enough water to cover, boil potatoes for 10 minutes. Let cool, then peel and cut into large chunks.

Preheat oven to 400 degrees F. Coat a 9- x 12-inch baking pan with 1 teaspoon of the butter.

Arrange potato and apple chunks in a single layer in pan. Combine brown sugar, salt, cinnamon, and allspice. Sprinkle over potatoes and apples. Dot with remaining butter. Bake 45 to 55 minutes, until potatoes are tender. Serve hot.

SERVES 4

Apples for Baking and Cooking
An apple that keeps its shape and flavor with exposure to heat is good for baking. Some excellent choices are Granny Smith, Golden Delicious, and Jonagold. Of course, the Rome Beauty built its reputation on its baking qualities.

APPLE-CORN BREAD STUFFING

Corn and apples make a terrific all-American combination for stuffing that Thanksgiving turkey.

1 tablespoon vegetable oil
1/2 pound loose mild sausage
2 onions, chopped
1/2 cup thinly sliced celery
4 Granny Smith apples, peeled, cored, and
   cut in 3/4-inch cubes
2 tablespoons chopped fresh sage
1 (16-ounce) package corn bread stuffing
1/2 cup chopped pecans
3/4 cup apple juice *or* cider
3/4 cup chicken broth
salt and freshly ground pepper

Preheat oven to 350 degrees F.

In large skillet, heat oil over medium-high heat. Sauté sausage, onions, and celery, stirring frequently, until sausage is browned, about 8 minutes. Stir in apples and sage, and cook, stirring, 5 minutes longer.

Transfer to large bowl. Add corn bread, pecans, apple juice, and broth. Toss to combine. Season to taste with salt and pepper. Transfer to casserole, cover, and bake 30 minutes. Uncover and bake 15 minutes longer.

SERVES 12

An American Legend
Johnny Appleseed, born John Chapman in Massachusetts in 1774, was a patriot, missionary, and nurseryman. Known for his eccentric ways, he gave sapling trees to pioneers headed west, and wandered as far west as Ohio and Indiana himself, preaching along the way as he planted and cared for apple orchards.

POTATO PANCAKES
WITH GOAT CHEESE AND APPLE

These savory little pancakes are an excellent finger food for a holiday buffet.

1 tablespoon butter
1 large Granny Smith apple, peeled, cored, and thinly sliced
2 eggs
$\frac{1}{4}$ cup heavy cream
$\frac{1}{4}$ cup all-purpose flour
1 tablespoon diced onion
1 large baking potato, peeled and finely shredded
salt and freshly ground pepper
2 tablespoons vegetable oil
4 ounces soft goat cheese, cut in 8 slices

Preheat the broiler.

In a small skillet, melt butter over low heat. Sauté the apple slices about 5 minutes and reserve.

In a bowl, whisk together eggs, cream, flour, and onion. Add potato, salt, and pepper, and mix well.

Heat oil in a medium skillet over medium-high heat. Drop in the potato batter by $\frac{1}{4}$-cupfuls, and press to flatten. Fry until golden, about 3 minutes per side. Transfer pancakes to a baking sheet. Top each with a goat cheese slice, and place under the broiler. Cook until cheese is hot and melted. Transfer pancakes to platter, and top each with sautéed apple slices. Serve warm.

SERVES 4

To Wax or Not to Wax
When apples are washed at the farm to remove dirt and chemicals, the fruit's natural coating is also removed. To compensate, a natural wax or shellac coating is applied to improve firmness, color, and shine and to slow aging.

GOLDEN APPLE
AND CARROT SLAW

When making this crunchy slaw, adjust the amount of sour cream and mayonnaise to suit your taste.

½ small green cabbage, shredded
2 large carrots, peeled and grated
2 large unpeeled Golden Delicious apples,
   grated
½ cup golden raisins
grated zest of 1 lemon
1 tablespoon fresh lemon juice
½ cup each sour cream and mayonnaise
salt and freshly ground pepper

In a large bowl, combine cabbage, carrots, apples, raisins, lemon zest, and juice. In another bowl, stir together sour cream and mayonnaise to blend. Pour over slaw mixture, and toss to evenly coat. Chill. Season to taste with salt and pepper.

SERVES 6 TO 8

HAROSET

This dish of chopped apples and walnuts is a symbolic food at the traditional Jewish Passover meal, or seder. Haroset is delicious spread on matzo or crackers.

2 Fuji, Gala, *or* Granny Smith apples, peeled, cored, and diced
$3/4$ cup walnuts, coarsely chopped
$1/4$ cup raisins, chopped
$1/2$ teaspoon ground cinnamon
$1 1/2$ tablespoons honey
juice of 1 lemon
1 tablespoon sweet red wine

Combine all of the ingredients in a bowl. Mix well, and reserve in the refrigerator up to a day.

MAKES 2 CUPS, ENOUGH FOR 4 TO 6

WHOLESOME
BREADS
AND
SNACKS

WARM GOAT CHEESE
AND APPLE SANDWICH

One of Helene's favorite quick lunches is this open-faced sandwich.

1 (10-inch) sourdough baguette
1 cup softened goat cheese
2 teaspoons honey
1 unpeeled Granny Smith apple, cored,
   quartered, and thinly sliced

Cut bread into two 5-inch lengths, and split lengthwise. Spread each with about ¼ cup of the cheese.

Place bread in toaster oven and top-brown only, or place on tray under broiler briefly to melt the cheese. Drizzle each with ½ teaspoon of honey, and top with layer of apple slices. Serve warm.

SERVES 2

APPLESAUCE SPICE MUFFINS

These lovely brown muffins get their extra moistness from the diced apple and sauce inside. Their fragrance comes from the cinnamon topping.

1³/₄ cups all-purpose flour
2¹/₂ teaspoons baking powder
1¹/₂ teaspoons cinnamon
¹/₂ teaspoon salt
¹/₄ teaspoon ground cloves
2 eggs
¹/₂ cup plus 2 tablespoons brown sugar
¹/₄ cup vegetable oil
¹/₂ cup milk
1 cup diced, peeled Golden Delicious *or*
    Fuji apple
1 tablespoon lemon juice
¹/₂ cup applesauce
¹/₂ teaspoon cinnamon mixed with
    3 tablespoons sugar, for topping

Preheat oven to 375 degrees F. Grease muffin tins, or line with paper cups.

In a medium bowl, combine flour, baking powder, cinnamon, salt, and cloves.

In another large bowl, whisk together eggs, brown sugar, oil, milk, apple, lemon juice, and applesauce. Add flour mixture to liquid ingredients. Stir just until flour disappears.

Spoon into muffin cups. Sprinkle tops with cinnamon sugar and bake 25 to 30 minutes, until tester comes out clean. Cool on rack. Invert to remove from pan, and serve.

MAKES 12

"He who will not a wife wed
Must eat an apple on going to bed."
          —old English saying

APPLE BROWN BREAD

Guests are sure to feel virtuous while munching away on this nutrition-packed apple-and-nut bread.

- $\frac{1}{2}$ stick butter, softened
- $\frac{1}{3}$ cup brown sugar
- 1 egg
- $\frac{1}{3}$ cup dark molasses
- 1 cup all-purpose flour
- 1 cup graham flour
- 1 teaspoon baking soda
- $\frac{1}{2}$ teaspoon baking powder
- $\frac{1}{2}$ teaspoon salt
- 1 cup buttermilk
- 1 cup diced, unpeeled Golden Delicious apple
- $\frac{1}{2}$ cup chopped walnuts

Preheat oven to 350 degrees F. Butter and flour a 9- x 5- x 3-inch loaf pan.

In a large bowl, cream together butter and brown sugar until light and fluffy. Beat in egg, then molasses (mixture may appear curdled).

In another bowl, combine two flours, baking soda and powder, and salt. Add flour mixture and buttermilk to creamed mixture in two parts, alternating liquid and dry and beating between additions. Gently stir in apple and walnuts.

Transfer batter to prepared pan and bake 1 hour 15 minutes, or until tester inserted in center comes out clean. Cool in pan 10 minutes. Turn out onto rack, and cool completely.

MAKES 1 LOAF

GRILLED APPLE REUBENS

Here is one for vegetarians who like their sandwiches sloppy—a meatless reuben!

8 slices rye bread
butter
Thousand Island dressing
8 slices Swiss cheese
1 (8-ounce) can sauerkraut, well drained
2 Red Delicious *or* McIntosh apples, cored
and thinly sliced into rings

Lightly spread one side of each bread slice with butter. Spread other sides with dressing. Heat griddle or large skillet at medium-high.

Place four bread slices, buttered-sides down, on griddle. Add one slice cheese, sauerkraut, a few apple slices, then remaining cheese. Top each with a slice of bread, buttered-side up. Cook until bottom is browned and crisp. Turn, and cook until bread is browned and cheese is melted. Cut in half and serve warm.

SERVES 4

Snack Apples
Any apple will do for munching out of hand or serving on a cheese platter, but Red Delicious, Granny Smith, Fuji, Braeburn, and Criterion really shine.

The Apple Plant

The apple, a member of the rose family, is the oldest cultivated fruit tree. It dates back to prehistoric times, and though there is disagreement over whether Adam and Eve actually ate an apple, apple trees were cultivated during biblical times. Evidence of apples has been found in the Nile delta and in ancient Greek and Roman ruins.

Believed to be a native of the Caucasus mountains of western Asia, the apple tree is an excellent example of a food plant that prospered and multiplied when brought to the New World. Apples need cool nights and days that are sunny but not too hot. America's best apple-growing states are Washington, New York, Michigan, Pennsylvania, California, Virginia, and North Carolina, with most of the nation's crop coming from Washington. The U.S. produces one-quarter of the world's supply.

APPLE CAKES, TARTS, AND PIES

GREEN APPLE CRISP

One of our favorite memories of visiting England is eating this homey dish for breakfast, with a little pitcher of cold cream.

4 large Granny Smith apples, peeled, cored, and quartered
1 tablespoon brandy *or* lemon juice
$\frac{1}{2}$ cup all-purpose flour
$\frac{1}{2}$ cup oatmeal
$\frac{1}{2}$ cup brown sugar
$\frac{1}{4}$ teaspoon cinnamon
pinch of salt
5 tablespoons butter, softened and cut in 12 pieces
$\frac{1}{2}$ cup pecans, lightly toasted and chopped
vanilla ice cream *or* heavy cream, for serving

Preheat oven to 375 degrees F. Lightly butter a 9-inch round pie plate or cake pan.

Slice each apple quarter into three wedges and place in bowl. Sprinkle with brandy and set aside.

In another bowl, combine flour, oatmeal, sugar, cinnamon, and salt. Pinching and rubbing lightly with fingertips or pastry blender, work butter into flour mixture until a crumbly mixture is formed. Lightly mix in nuts by hand.

Layer apples into prepared pan. Evenly sprinkle crumb mixture over all. Bake about 40 minutes, until top is brown and apples soft. Serve hot with vanilla ice cream or cold heavy cream.

SERVES 6

APPLE BLUEBERRY CRUMBLE TART

A warm slice of this tender tart, topped with a dollop of plain yogurt, makes a heavenly breakfast.

1 recipe "Shortbread Tart Crust" (see page 74) or prepared pie crust
4 small Golden Delicious apples, peeled, cored, and sliced
1 cup blueberries
2 tablespoons lemon juice
$1/4$ cup sugar
$1/4$ teaspoon cinnamon

CRUMBLE TOPPING
$1/3$ cup brown sugar
$1/2$ stick butter, softened
$1/4$ teaspoon cinnamon
pinch of nutmeg and salt
$3/4$ cup all-purpose flour

Preheat oven to 375 degrees F. Roll out the dough to 10-inch circle, and line a 9-inch round tart pan. Prick all over with a fork, line with foil and weights (rice or beans), and bake 15 minutes. Remove weights.

Meanwhile, toss together the apples, blueberries, lemon juice, sugar, and cinnamon in a bowl.

In another bowl, make the topping. Cream together sugar, butter, cinnamon, nutmeg, and salt until fluffy. Gently mix in flour just until crumbly.

Spoon apple mixture into partially baked tart shell, leaving liquid in bowl. Sprinkle crumble topping evenly over fruit, and bake 45 to 55 minutes, until crust is golden-brown. Serve warm or at room temperature.

SERVES 8

"The apple of my eye."
        —*popular expression*

TARTE TATIN

The famous upside-down caramelized apple tart always tastes better at home, where it can be brought to the table in all its browned glory, straight from the oven.

1 stick butter
¾ cup sugar
12 Golden Delicious apples, peeled, cored, and quartered
1 sheet (about ½ pound) frozen puff pastry, thawed
Whipped cream *or* vanilla ice cream, for serving

In a 10-inch skillet with ovenproof handle, cook the butter and sugar over medium heat until melted. Remove from heat.

Arrange all the apples upright in a spiral pattern in the pan. Place over medium-low heat and cook, uncovered, without stirring, about 1 hour 20 minutes. The liquid in the pan should be brown and bubbly. Let cool 10 minutes.

Preheat the oven to 375 degrees F.

Roll out the pastry on a floured board into a 12-inch circle. Place over the apples in the pan, tucking in excess dough. Immediately transfer to the oven and bake about 30 minutes, until pastry is puffed and golden. Cool 20 minutes. To serve, place a large serving platter over the pan, quickly invert, and lift the pan. Rearrange apples to smooth the top, and spoon on any extra caramel sauce from pan. Serve warm with whipped cream or vanilla ice cream, if desired.

SERVES 8 TO 10

"The apple was the first fruit of the world, according to Genesis, but it was no Cox's orange pippin. God gave the crab apple and left the rest to man."
    —Jane Grigson

APPLE PANDOWDY

Pandowdy, with its sloppy broken top crust, is great for novice bakers.

butter for coating
4 Granny Smith apples, peeled, cored, and
   sliced
2 tablespoons lemon juice
$\frac{1}{2}$ cup maple syrup
1 teaspoon allspice
1 frozen (9-inch) pie crust, thawed
1 tablespoon melted butter, for glaze
1 tablespoon sugar mixed with $\frac{1}{4}$ teaspoon
   cinnamon, for glaze

Preheat oven to 400 degrees F. Lightly coat a 9-inch pie pan with butter.

In a bowl, combine the apples, lemon juice, maple syrup, and allspice and mix well. Transfer to pie pan. Unfold the pie dough, and place over the apples, tucking the edges into pan. Brush top with melted butter and sprinkle with cinnamon sugar. With a paring knife, cut four vents in pastry. Bake for $1/2$ hour. Remove from oven, and reduce heat to 350 degrees F.

With the paring knife, cut pastry into a 1-inch checkerboard. With a slotted spoon, press broken pastry into filling. Bake $1/2$ hour longer, removing once to press down topping again. Spoon into bowls and serve hot.

SERVES 6

"American as apple pie."
    —folk expression

ALL-AMERICAN APPLE PIE

So what if it's a culinary cliché? Absolutely nothing beats a slice of double-crusted, browned-on-top, straight-from-the-oven, warm and tender all-American apple pie–our hands-down favorite coffee accompaniment.

6 Granny Smith apples, peeled, cored, and
    cut in large chunks
2 tablespoons lemon juice
$^3/_4$ cup sugar
1 teaspoon cinnamon
$^1/_4$ teaspoon allspice
2 tablespoons cornstarch
2 (9-inch) prepared pie crusts or "All-
    American Pie Crust" (see page 72)
1 egg white, lightly beaten
sugar, for sprinkling

Preheat oven to 425 degrees F.

In a large bowl, combine apples, lemon juice, sugar, cinnamon, allspice, and cornstarch. Toss well.

On a floured board, lightly roll out one piece of dough into a 12-inch circle, dusting top as needed. (Patch rips with a few drops of water and extra flour.) Line a 9-inch pie pan, brushing off excess flour and building up the edges. Fill center with apple mixture. Brush the top edge of the dough with egg white. Roll out the second dough disk. Carefully place over the apples, and press the edges together to seal. Crimp the edge or press with tines of a fork. Brush top with egg white and sprinkle with sugar. With a paring knife, cut about four 1-inch slits to vent steam.

Bake 10 minutes on lower rack. Reduce heat to 350 degrees F and bake another 60 to 70 minutes, until the juices are bubbling and top is golden-brown. Cool on rack 1 hour.

MAKES 1 PIE

INDIVIDUAL HOT APPLE TARTS

With frozen puff pastry and a dash of apple brandy, you too can create an authentic French restaurant dessert at home.

> 6 tablespoons butter
> 6 Granny Smith apples, peeled, cored, and thinly sliced
> ½ cup sugar
> 2 tablespoons apple brandy (such as calvados)
> 1 pound frozen puff pastry, thawed

Preheat oven to 400 degrees F.

In a large saucepan, melt butter over medium-high heat. Add the apples and sugar, and cook, stirring frequently, until golden, about 10 minutes.

Place half the apple slices in blender or food processor. Add brandy, and purée. Chill, along with remaining slices, for ½ hour.

Roll out pastry to ¼-inch thickness. With floured cutter or glass, cut pastry into six 4-inch circles, and place on uncoated baking sheets. Spread each with apple purée, leaving ½ inch bare along the edge. Arrange apple slices in a fan over each. Bake 35 to 40 minutes, until pastry is puffed and brown. Serve hot.

SERVES 6

The Washington Apple
Washington state produces more than half the U.S. apple crop—230 to 250 million boxes a year. In addition to feeding Americans, those apples make it into lunchboxes and fruit bowls in Asia, South America, and Canada. The original Washington apple seed was brought west by Captain Aemilus Simpson and planted in Fort Vancouver in 1824. It came from an apple brought from London.

QUICK APPLE TART

This unfussy free-form tart, called a galette *in France, makes a delicious dessert with a scoop of vanilla ice cream or a splash of* crème fraîche. *For the next day's breakfast, just reheat and top with a dollop of plain yogurt.*

1 cup all-purpose flour
1 teaspoon plus ¼ cup sugar
pinch of salt
6 tablespoons cold butter, cut in slices
2 tablespoons cold water
3 large Golden Delicious apples, peeled, halved lengthwise, cored, and thinly sliced in semicircles

In a food processor with metal blade, combine flour, teaspoon of sugar, and salt. Pulse to combine. Add butter, and pulse briefly just until mixture resembles coarse meal. Add the water, and pulse a few times until pastry holds together when pressed. Transfer to work surface, press into a disk, and wrap in plastic. Chill for ½ hour to 2 days.

Preheat oven to 400 degrees F. Butter and flour a heavy baking or cookie sheet.

On a lightly floured board, roll out the dough to a 10-inch circle. Carefully transfer to prepared sheet. Gently build up the edges with your hands to shape a free-form crust. Brush off excess flour. Arrange apple slices in circular pattern over dough. Sprinkle with ¼ cup sugar and bake 1 hour and 10 minutes, until crust is golden brown and apples are brown on edges. Cool, and transfer with spatula to serving platter. Cut in wedges and serve warm or cold.

SERVES 6 TO 8

"An apple pie without some cheese is like a kiss without a squeeze."

—*proverb*

APPLE BROWN BETTY

Those frugal New Englanders knew how to pull together a few simple ingredients to make a very warm and cozy dessert dish like this brown Betty.

2 cups coarse, dry, homemade bread crumbs
6 tablespoons butter, melted
3 large Granny Smith *or* McIntosh apples, peeled, cored, and sliced into thick wedges
3/4 cup brown sugar
1 teaspoon cinnamon
1/4 teaspoon nutmeg
juice and grated zest of 1/2 lemon
1/3 cup apple cider
vanilla ice cream *or* frozen yogurt

Preheat oven to 350 degrees F. Grease 8-inch-square baking dish.

In a small bowl, toss together bread crumbs and butter. In another bowl, toss apples with brown sugar, cinnamon, nutmeg, lemon juice, and zest. Spread about a third of the crumb mixture in bottom of prepared dish. Top with half of apple mixture and another layer of crumbs, then the remaining apples and a final layer of crumbs. Pour in apple cider.

Cover with foil and bake 20 minutes. Uncover and bake 20 minutes longer, or until browned on top. Serve with ice cream or yogurt, if desired.

SERVES 6

GINGERBREAD APPLE UPSIDE-DOWN CAKE

When it's time to pull out all the stops and wow those unsuspecting guests, serve this caramelized sugar and apple cake topped with spicy ginger cream.

8 tablespoons butter, half melted and
    half softened
½ cup brown sugar
1 teaspoon cinnamon
2 Golden Delicious *or* Pink Lady apples, cored
    and sliced into wedges
⅓ cup granulated sugar
1 egg
⅓ cup molasses
⅓ cup apple cider
1¼ cups all-purpose flour
1 teaspoon ground ginger
1 teaspoon baking soda
½ teaspoon salt
1 tablespoon finely chopped crystallized ginger
1 cup heavy cream, whipped

Preheat oven to 350 degrees F.

Coat a 9-inch round cake pan with the melted butter. Combine brown sugar and cinnamon, and sprinkle evenly over butter. Starting in center of pan, arrange apple slices in concentric overlapping circles over bottom. Set aside.

In a large bowl, cream together softened butter and granulated sugar. Beat in egg, molasses, and cider (mixture may appear curdled). In another bowl, sift together flour, ginger, baking soda, and salt. Stir into creamed mixture until smooth. Slowly pour batter over apples. Bake 30 minutes. Cool in pan 10 minutes.

To serve, invert cake onto platter, spooning on excess sugar from pan. Fold crystallized ginger into whipped cream. Serve warm cake with flavored cream.

MAKES 1 CAKE, ABOUT 8 SERVINGS

ALL-AMERICAN PIE CRUST

Here is the standard American crust that shatters into flakes.

2½ cups all-purpose flour
2 teaspoons sugar
½ teaspoon salt
1 stick butter, cold, cut in ½-inch slices
½ cup shortening, cold, in tablespoon-size
   pieces
6 tablespoons cold water

In a large mixing bowl, combine flour, sugar, and salt. Add butter and shortening. Combine by pinching with fingertips or pastry blender until fat is evenly distributed and broken into hazelnut-size pieces. (The mixture should hold together when pressed.) Add water all at once, and stir a few times with wooden spoon. Turn out onto plastic wrap, and loosely wrap. Gently knead into a ball and then divide in half. Covering each with plastic, press each into 5-inch disk and wrap well. Chill from 1 hour to 3 days or freeze for later use.

MAKES TWO (9-INCH) PIE CRUSTS

That Pie Thing

It takes approximately 2½ pounds—five large or seven to eight medium apples—to fill the typical 9-inch round all-American pie pan. But more important—which apple to use? On this controversial question we prefer staying with the tried and true: Granny Smith, Golden Delicious, or Newtown Pippin. Although they're lovely to contemplate, steer away from those crisp, new Fujis or Galas. They don't stand up to lengthy baking in a pie.

SHORTBREAD TART CRUST

This is an extra-tender and crumbly crust.

1¼ cups cake flour
½ cup confectioners' sugar
pinch of salt
6 tablespoons butter, cold, cut in pieces
1 egg yolk beaten with ½ teaspoon vanilla

In a food processor fitted with the metal blade, combine flour, sugar, and salt. Pulse to mix. Add butter, and pulse to break into small pieces. Add yolk mixture. Pulse until mixture is crumbly and holds together when pressed. Transfer to sheet of plastic wrap, press into disk, wrap, and chill 1 hour.

MAKES ONE 9- OR 10-INCH TART

Apples in All Their Variety

There are some 7,500 varieties of apples in the world today. The U.S. produces about three hundred different types, and of those about twenty constitute the commercial market. The best sellers, in descending order, are Red Delicious, Golden Delicious, McIntosh, Granny Smith, Fuji, and Gala.

Though older varieties such as Delicious and Grannies began cultivation naturally as seedlings that produced fruit that people tasted and liked, the apple business has grown a bit more precise about marketing new products. It now takes about ten years of experimentation to bring a new variety to market. Farmers aren't just hoping to capture America's taste buds with each new apple—they also want fruit that stores well and doesn't burn in the sun. Happily, American consumers are looking for more and more choices in everything, including their apples.

SWEET TREATS
AND
BEVERAGES

APPLE BREAD PUDDING WITH HARD CIDER SAUCE

Skip the bourbon-and-cider (or hard liquor) sauce if you must. Either way, this rich apple pudding is reason enough to finish a meal.

2 cups half-and-half
2 eggs plus 2 yolks
⅓ cup brown sugar
2 teaspoons cinnamon
¼ teaspoon salt
1 teaspoon vanilla
4 cups day-old white bread cubes, crusts trimmed
2 cups peeled Gala *or* Fuji apple cubes
½ cup golden raisins
Hard Cider Sauce (see next page)

Butter an 8-inch-square baking dish.

In large bowl, whisk together half-and-half, eggs, egg yolks, brown sugar, cinnamon, salt, and vanilla. Add bread cubes, apples, and raisins, and toss to coat thoroughly. Let stand 15 minutes.

Preheat oven to 350 degrees F.

Pour mixture into prepared dish. Place dish in larger pan filled with water to halfway up sides of baking dish. Bake 50 minutes. Cool slightly. Serve warm with Hard Cider Sauce.

SERVES 8

HARD CIDER SAUCE

- ½ cup sugar
- 2 egg yolks
- ¼ cup apple cider
- 2 tablespoons bourbon
- 4 tablespoons butter, cut into 8 pieces and softened

In top of a double boiler, whisk sugar and egg yolks until light. Set over simmering water, and whisk in cider and bourbon. Cook, whisking constantly, until mixture is hot and slightly thickened, about 3 minutes.

Remove from heat, and whisk in butter until completely melted. Serve hot.

The Americanization of the Apple
Apple seeds were brought to the colonies by English, French, German, and Dutch settlers. The first orchard was planted in Boston in 1625 by William Blaxton, an English preacher. In 1647, Peter Stuyvesant, the Dutch governor of New York, planted an orchard at his farm in New York's Bowery. Two years later, apples had enough value for Governor John Endicott of Plymouth colony to trade five hundred apple trees for two hundred acres of land. About one hundred years later, America was exporting apples to the Old World with a shipment to London of Newtown Pippins for Benjamin Franklin. By the 19th century, Queen Victoria of England lifted a ban on American-grown fruit to let in those irresistible Pippins. The word "apple" is derived from the English oeppel. And apple pie as we know it is a British creation.

MAPLE-APPLE ICE CREAM

A superb fresh-fruit ice cream like this is the best reason we can think of to take out that dusty, old ice-cream maker.

4 egg yolks
3 cups heavy cream
1 cup milk
3/4 cup sugar
1/2 cup maple syrup
2 tablespoons butter
2 Golden Delicious *or* Pink Lady apples, peeled, cored, and thinly sliced
1 teaspoon ground ginger
1/2 cup toasted pecans *or* walnuts

In a small bowl, whisk egg yolks until slightly thickened.

In a saucepan, combine cream, milk, sugar, and 1/4 cup of the maple syrup. Bring to gentle boil over medium-high heat, stirring to dissolve sugar. Whisk about 1 cup hot mixture into yolks, then whisk yolk mixture back into pan. Cook over medium-low heat, stirring constantly, until mixture is thick enough to coat back of spoon, about 5 minutes. Pour through fine sieve into large bowl. Cool slightly, then cover with plastic wrap, and refrigerate at least 4 hours.

Meanwhile, melt butter in skillet over medium-high heat. Add apples and ginger, and sauté just until tender and beginning to brown, about 5 minutes. Add remaining $1/4$ cup syrup and nuts, and cook for 2 minutes, stirring often. Set aside to cool.

Freeze cream mixture in ice-cream maker according to manufacturer's instructions, adding apple mixture at end. Transfer ice cream to freezer container, cover tightly, and freeze for at least 2 hours before serving.

MAKES ABOUT $1^1/2$ QUARTS

BAKED APPLES MANHATTAN

An old favorite is brought up to the moment with dried cherries and sweet vermouth.

6 large Golden Delicious *or* Pink Lady apples
6 tablespoons sugar
6 tablespoons dried cherries
2 tablespoons butter
grated zest of 1 orange
$1/2$ cup apple cider
$1/2$ cup bourbon
2 tablespoons sweet vermouth

Preheat oven to 350 degrees F.

Core apples, leaving bottoms intact. Peel top third of apples. Place in large baking dish, cut-side up.

Combine sugar and cherries, and spoon into apple cavities. Dot with butter. Scatter orange zest around apples. Pour in cider, bourbon, and vermouth. Cover and bake 30 minutes. Uncover and bake 15 minutes

longer, or until apples are tender.
Serve warm, spooning any sauce in pan
over apples.

SERVES 6

Moments in Apple History

- *Eve tempts Adam with a fruit from the Tree of Knowledge (could be a quince, could be an apple, who really knows?), thereby causing humankind's expulsion from Eden.*
- *Her evil stepmother foists a poison apple on unsuspecting ingenue Snow White. After a nice, long sleep, she wakes up and marries a prince.*
- *Swiss patriot and archer William Tell proves a point by shooting an apple off his son's head.*
- *Isaac Newton observes an apple fall from a tree, and the idea of gravity is born.*
- *A group of geeks get together in someone's garage, take the name Apple, and give birth to a tabletop computer called Macintosh.*

GRANDMA'S BAKED APPLES

This was Helene's grandmother Yetta's favorite dessert—minus the Grand Marnier, of course. Gussy it up with vanilla ice cream or a spoonful of honey, or take it straight-up as Grandma did.

4 large Rome apples
2½ tablespoons brown sugar
¼ teaspoon cinnamon
1 tablespoon butter
¼ cup Grand Marnier *or* apple brandy
¼ cup apple cider

Preheat oven to 375 degrees F. Peel top halves of apples and remove the cores, leaving bottoms intact. Place in baking dish, cut-side up.

Combine the sugar and cinnamon. Divide in four and stuff into apple centers. Top each with a pat of butter. Mix together Grand Marnier, or brandy, and cider. Drizzle over the apples. Bake until tender, about 1 hour, basting during the last $\frac{1}{2}$ hour. Cool slightly before serving.

SERVES 4

"All millionaires love a baked apple."
    —English author Ronald Firbank

CARAMEL APPLES

You may remember these sticky brown treats from Halloween or outdoor fairs.

6 wooden skewers *or* popsicle sticks
6 apples
1½ pounds caramel candies
3 tablespoons water
chopped nuts, chocolate chips, toasted
   coconut, raisins, *or* chopped dried fruit
   for topping (optional)

Line baking sheet with waxed paper. Remove stems from apples, and insert skewer in stem end of each.

Combine caramels and water in top of double boiler over simmering water. Heat, stirring often, until caramels are melted and mixture is smooth. Dip apples into mixture one at a time, covering entire fruit. Remove, scraping off excess caramel on pan's edge. Place, with stick up, on prepared baking sheet, and cool. If desired, roll apples in topping while still warm and soft.

MAKES 6

"My wife's and my supper half the year consists of apple pie and milk."

> —*Michel-Guillaume Jean de Crèvecoeur, a French writer living in New York after the French Revolution*

DUTCH BABY APPLE PANCAKE

The apple topping and batter can be prepared hours before guests arrive. For an impressive dessert, just reheat topping and pop the pancake in the oven when dinner is finished.

5 tablespoons butter
3 apples, peeled, cored, and sliced
$\frac{1}{4}$ cup maple syrup
1 tablespoon plus 2 teaspoons lemon juice
$\frac{1}{4}$ teaspoon cinnamon
2 eggs
$\frac{1}{2}$ cup all-purpose flour
$\frac{1}{2}$ cup milk
$\frac{1}{2}$ teaspoon vanilla

Preheat oven to 400 degrees F.

Melt 2 tablespoons of the butter in a large skillet over medium-high heat. Sauté apples until golden, about 8 minutes. Add maple syrup, lemon juice, and cinnamon, and reduce heat to low. Cook, stirring occasionally, until tender but not mushy, 15 to 20 minutes. Set aside.

In a bowl, whisk together eggs, flour, milk, and vanilla.

In an ovenproof 10-inch skillet, melt the remaining butter over medium-high heat. Pour in the batter, swirl to coat evenly, and place in oven. Bake about 15 minutes, until golden and puffed—the peak in the center will deflate. Transfer to serving platter with spatula, top with sautéed apples, and cut into wedges to serve.

SERVES 4

SWEET APPLE FRITTERS

Dust these lightly fried treats with sugar and serve after the meal, or try them plain as a side dish with roasted or braised meats.

1 egg
1 1/2 teaspoons sugar
1/3 cup milk
1 cup all-purpose flour
1/2 teaspoon baking powder
1/4 teaspoon salt
vegetable oil for deep frying
2 large Golden Delicious *or* Pink Lady
    apples, peeled, cored, and sliced into
    1/4-inch-thick rings
confectioners' sugar *or* maple syrup,
    for serving

In a medium bowl, beat egg and sugar together. Stir in milk. In another bowl, combine flour, baking powder, and salt. Add to liquid and stir to blend.

Preheat oven to 250 degrees F. In deep pot or fryer, heat about 2 inches oil to 375 degrees F.

Dip apple slices into batter, draining excess back into bowl. Carefully drop slices into hot oil, frying about six slices at a time. Fry until golden, about 2 minutes each side. Remove with slotted spoon, and drain on paper towels. Transfer to baking sheet and keep warm in oven until done. Serve warm with confectioners' sugar or syrup.

SERVES 4

"Huge, hard apples with cheeks beginning to blush were everywhere, and their fragrance was so powerful that I could smell them as soon as I saw them."
　　　—*Greg Atkinson*

GREEN APPLE GRANITA

This thick, granular slush is a shortcut sorbet. You don't need an ice cream maker to make it—a food processor will do.

1 cup sugar
1 cup water
1 tablespoon honey
3 Granny Smith apples, peeled, cored, and roughly chopped
¼ cup marsala wine
2 tablespoons apple brandy (such as calvados)
2 tablespoons lemon juice

In a small pot, combine sugar, water, and honey. Bring to a boil, reduce to a simmer, and cook 10 minutes. Let cool.

Transfer apples to food processor. Add remaining ingredients and sugar syrup. Purée until creamy. Pour into 10-inch round metal cake pan, and place in freezer to set, about

4 hours. Remove from freezer and let sit 5 minutes to soften. Break into pieces with blunt knife, and transfer to food processor. Pulse until granular slush is formed. Transfer to a plastic container and store in the freezer, or serve immediately.

MAKES ABOUT 1 QUART

Commercial Storage
Apple varieties like Red Delicious are available all year round thanks to Controlled Atmosphere Storage—a process that slows ripening. Unripe apples, picked and boxed at just the right time, are stored in sealed rooms with reduced oxygen and controlled carbon dioxide levels, 95 percent humidity, and a temperature between 32 and 36 degrees. In controlled storage, apples can keep as long as a year. Favorites for cold storage are Red and Golden Delicious, McIntosh, Rome Beauty, and Granny Smith.

HOT APPLE TODDY

An alcohol-free toddy to warm your insides without fogging the head.

3 cups apple cider
2- to 3-inch piece lemon peel
dash nutmeg
2 unpeeled McIntosh apple slices, cored and
  cut into half-circles
4 whole cloves
4 cinnamon sticks

In saucepan, combine apple cider, lemon peel, and nutmeg. Stud each apple half-circle with a clove. Add to pan along with cinnamon sticks. Bring to simmer. Cook 1 minute. Remove and discard lemon peel. Serve in cups, each with an apple slice and cinnamon stick.

SERVES 4

HOTTER APPLE TODDY

All you need is a warm fireplace and someone special to put the finishing touches on this hotter-than-hot toddy.

1 cup apple juice
3 cloves
dash each nutmeg and cinnamon
4 unpeeled Red Delicious *or* McIntosh apple
   wedges
¼ cup brandy
2 tablespoons Grand Marnier *or* other
   orange liqueur
2 cinnamon sticks for garnish

In saucepan, combine apple juice and spices. Bring to boil. Meanwhile, place two apple wedges in each of two mugs. Remove juice from heat, and stir in brandy and liqueur. Pour over apple wedges in mugs. Garnish with cinnamon sticks and serve hot.

SERVES 2

CONVERSIONS

LIQUID
1 Tbsp = 15 ml
½ cup = 4 fl oz = 125 ml
1 cup = 8 fl oz = 250 ml

DRY
¼ cup = 4 Tbsp = 2 oz = 60 g
1 cup = ½ pound = 8 oz = 250 g

FLOUR
½ cup = 60 g
1 cup = 4 oz = 125 g

TEMPERATURE
400° F = 200° C = gas mark 6
375° F = 190° C = gas mark 5
350° F = 175° C = gas mark 4

MISCELLANEOUS
2 Tbsp butter = 1 oz = 30 g
1 inch = 2.5 cm
all-purpose flour = plain flour
baking soda = bicarbonate of soda
brown sugar = demerara sugar
heavy cream = double cream
sugar = caster sugar